Editor's note: Most of the cartoons in this book were created to celebrate the annual Pro-Am golf tournament hosted by singer Bing Crosby (which continues today under AT$T's sponsorship.) If you see a few references to Bing or to the physical properties of the Pebble Beach golf courses where the "clambake" (as the tournament is affectionately known) takes place, that's why!

GUS ARRIOLA

Arizona-born **Gustavo Arriola** is best known as the creator of *Gordo*, a delightful comic strip known for its use of Mexican culture and the beauty of nature. Launched in 1941, *Gordo* ran for over forty years. *Peanuts* creator Charles M. Schulz once called Gordo "probably the most beautifully drawn strip in the history of the business."

GREAT GOLF GAGS BY CLASSIC CARTOONISTS

EDITED BY NAT GERTLER

ABOUT COMICS | CAMARILLO, CALIFORNIA

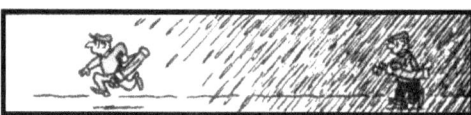

Great Golf Gags by Classic Cartoonists

Annotations created for this edition by About Comics.
Compilation copyright 2017 About Comics.

ISBN: 978-1-936404-73-5

Published October, 2017.

For bulk orders, custom covers, or other inquiries,
contact *questions@aboutcomics.com*

ELDON DEDINI

The lush single panel cartoons of native Californian **Eldon Dedin** (1921-2006) were a regular feature in such premiere outlets as *Esquire* and *Playboy*. He was awarded the National Cartoonist Society's Gag Cartoon Award four times, in three different decades. (One of his paintings provides the cover to this book.)

What's so funny?

"I understand this is considered the finest meeting of land and water in the world."

"Now you know why they call it the World Famous 16th Hole at Cypress Point."

"Comes the revolution and we'll **all** break par."

"My cholesterol count and golf game are now exactly the same."

"It soothes my wife. At least she knows I'm thinking of her"

"I've been paired with some wild amateurs, but this takes the cake!"

"I don't know what were in those pills my doctor gave me, but I've helped my Pro twenty strokes so far!"

"I know why I'm invited back each year, but why in the world are *you* invited back each year?"

"I shot 6 under par in my last movie—
thanks to my stunt man."

"No. I haven't seen a 1974 blue Fiat Spyder. Have you seen a white Titleist #4 golf ball?"

"Do my eyes deceive me or is he wearing last year's hat?"

HANK KETCHAM

Dennis the Menace creator **Henry Ketcham** (1920-2001) spent years before launching his famous daily panel working on Disney features like *Pinnochio* and *Bambi*, serving in the Navy Reserve, and doing magazine cartoons.

GUESS WHO'S THE PRO—In the game of golf it is sometimes difficult to tell who's who. In this case we present the usual twosome. The quiet, unassuming, scared looking chap is the professional, of course. While on the right we have our amateur, colorful, confident and ready for anything.

Emmet Fridley, popular pro at the Guano Country Club, Bird Rock, Calif., demonstrates perfect swing in this stop-action picture. Notice fixed position of head throughout. For secret of his perfect form, see opposite page.

Emmet Fridley reveals secret of perfect swing shown on facing page. "It's easy," he says. "Just keep your head down and swing with everything you've got!"

BILL O'MALLEY

While **Bill O'Malley** did a fair number of cartoons about people's habits like golf, he is better known for his cartoons about people *in* habits. His cartoons about the nuns Sister Maureen and Sister Colleen were popular in the 1950s and 1960s.

VIRGIL PARTCH

Virgil Franklin Partch (1916-1984) who (despite his middle name) often signed his work *Vip*, was such a prolific single-panel cartoonist that his series *Big George* continued to have new daily installments for six years after he died.

"Watch it Bing — I'm Blasting!"

Easy, Tex. He tees off at seven in the morning.

I've never taken a lesson.

There's another foursome coming up ... don't you think we'd better replace the pin?

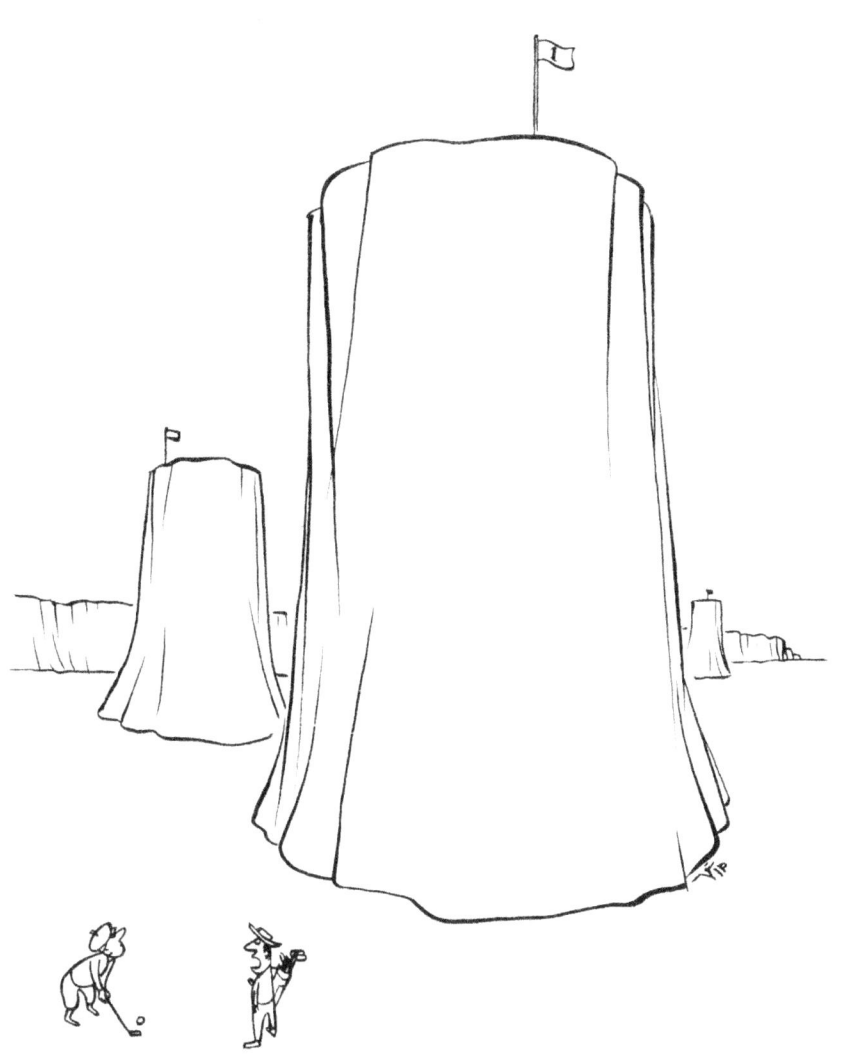

Watch it. The greens are like lightning today.

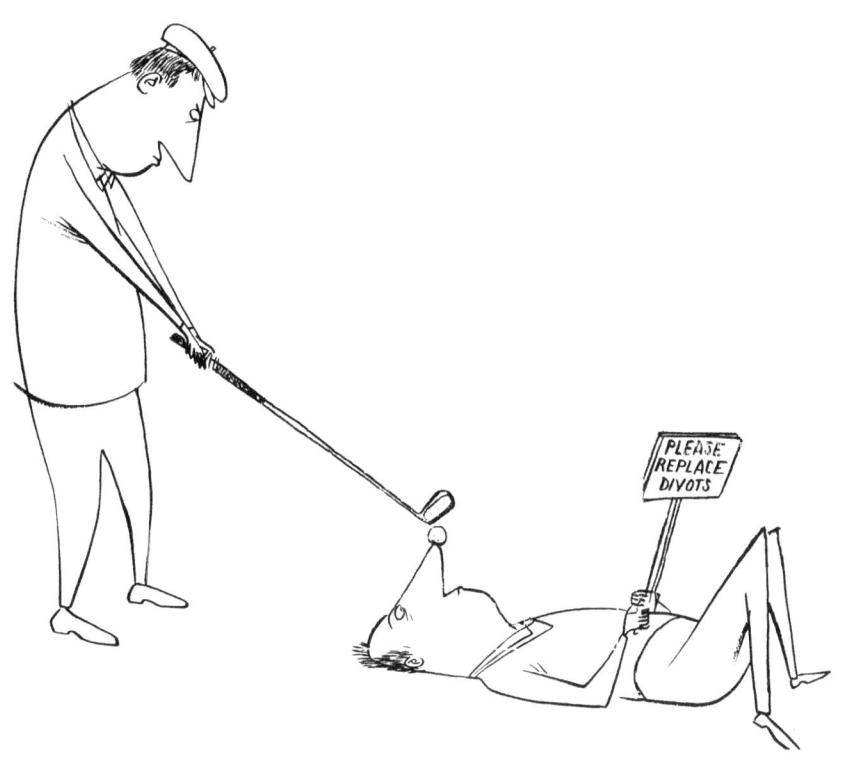

"Now there's a real golfer for you. Notice how he keeps that left arm straight, legs slightly bent..."

"Whatca' bitching about? The flag's practically in the middle of the green!"

"BOY, I THOUGHT MIDDLECOFF TOOK HIS TIME READING A GREEN!"

"He's obviously never read 'The Power of Positive Thinking'."

"No, the first guy's the pro. The one wearing the ice bag is his amateur partner."

"It'll break to your left"

CHARLES M. SCHULZ

The works of **Charles Monroe Schulz** (1922-2000), particularly the *Peanuts* characters he created, continue to have a huge presence in the world. An army veteran, Schulz had a history of doing single-panel cartoons for magazines and local papers before launching *Peanuts*, which he would craft for fifty years. (Some of the Schulz cartoons presented here have finished art by Jim Sasseville.)

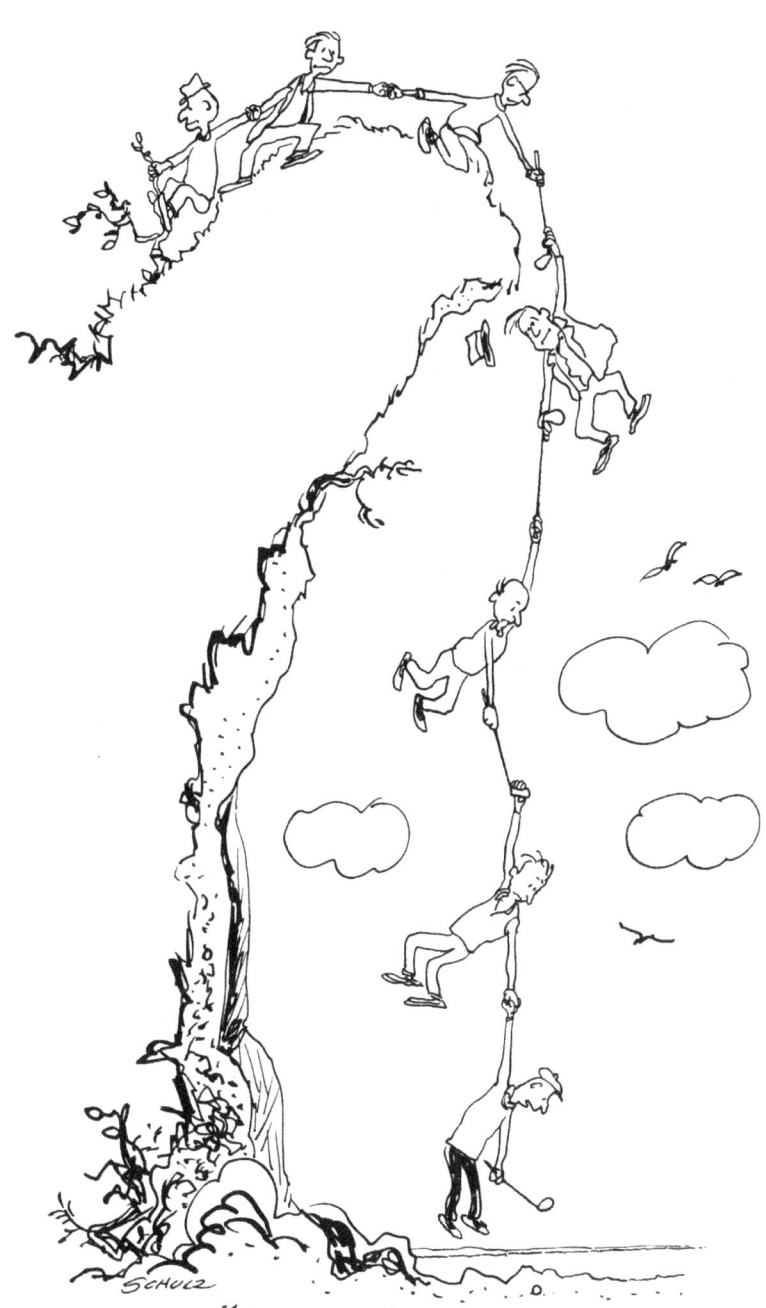

WE'LL GO OVER HERE TO THE SIXTH TEE, SLIDE DOWN THAT HILL PAST THE BIG SANDTRAP, AROUND THE DOG-LEG, AND UP TO THE FOURTH GREEN...

OTHER BOOKS FOR THE CLASSIC CARTOON FAN, FROM ABOUT COMICS

Charles M. Schulz takes on the game of bridge, and the people who play the game. These classic 1950s gag panels still bring joy today.

As seen in American Contract Bridge League publications

ASK FOR IT WHERE YOU GOT THIS BOOK!

ILLUSTRATED BY CHARLES M. SCHULZ

Kid's Letters to President Kennedy From the early days of the JFK administration comes this collection of letters from the youth of America, edited by Bill Adler (creator of the *New York Times* best=seller *The Kennedy Wit*, profusely illustrated by Silent Spring artist Louis Darling.
ISBN 978-1936404-61-2

Dear President Johnson reveals children's letters to LBJ, edited by *New York Times* best=seller Bill Adler, illustrated by Peanuts creator Charles M. Schulz.
ISBN 978-1936404-56-8

14 weeks on the *New York Times* Best-Seller list!
Out of print for half a century!
Now available in this expanded edition.
Illustrated by the great Mort Drucker

This biting political satire gives us a reminder of the Kennedy years, the way they were seen before he was given the mantle of martyrdom.

Ask for it where you got this book!